Songs And Poems

Rachel Lawson

Contents

Chapter 1
Tears of a Clown

I am Pierrot, don't call me a clown,

I bear the rose of a broken heart,

I lost my love to my rival,

So I cry, No, I do not lie,

Or will I lay down my rose, my heart.

My tears are my heart's lost blood,

I will die of grief before I lay down my rose,

My heart will die.

I am Pierrot, don't call me a clown,

I bear the rose of a broken heart,

I lost my love to my rival,

So I cry, No, I do not lie,

Or will I lay down my rose, my heart.

My tears are my heart's lost blood,

I will die of grief before I lay down my rose,

My heart will die.

Chapter 2
Take Me As I Am

Spoken passionate
I love you more than life,
and death won't end it, my love for you.

You gotta take me as I am,
I can't give you more than this,
I am just a poor man, nothing more can I give you,
All I have to give you is my love and my name,
I am not wealthy, but in love I am rich,
If I have your love,
I am the richest man in the world, with your love.
I can soar above the world,
With the hope you give me,
With your love and faith
I can do anything,
I could do anything you ask of me,
If you call me,
I would fly to your side,
You make me feel like I'm a superman,

your love makes me feel I can do anything,
The world and death can't stop my love for you,

You are an angel living in my heart,
I pray to you, that we will never part,
Spoken passionate
I love you!

Chapter 3
The Fall of Man

The moon has fallen,
The end of the world is callin',
Death is coming to the world,
In anarchy, the world is hurled,
All the king's horses and all the King's men can not put us together
again,
We have lost the world of men,
Our kingdom has fallen,
The world is dyin',
I am alone in the dark,
Lost in terror stark,
We are the last of our race.
We have lost life's chase.

Chapter 4

Dick Turpin & the King of the Road

Upon the road, Tom, the King of the road, met Turpin,

Dick thought Tom King was a fat pigeon,

they rode together on their way,

they robbed people with their guns under the code of the men of the

highway,

"Your money or your life?" they did call,

it was nothing or all,

Tom made Turpin a highwayman legend,

it was rumoured Turpin brought King to his end,

Tom was shot in the shoulder,

he was taken to the Doctor,

he could not be saved,

Turpin, goodbye to the road he waved,

a butcher he became,

he was caught under a charge of a poaching claim,

he wrote a letter for help from one of his in-laws,

the only problem was the letter his death did cause,

an old teacher of Turpin's read through his fraud,
they knew his handwriting he told the truth and no one could save
him not even the good Lord.
he was revealed and caught,
the gallows called according to the court.
death came swiftly,
the legend grew greater hereby quickly.

Chapter 5
Nevermore- song

Nevermore shall I see your face in this world,
I am lost and alone,
I miss your smile,
You are lost to the world,
Sleeping in the eternal sleep of death,
In your cold grave,
I kneel by your grave,
I feel nearer to you,
Even though we are far from each other,
Between us are life and death,
The furthest distance in space and time,
I reach in my dreams to see you,
To hear your voice again,
I reach out to you in my dreams,
Only to have you disappear like a wisp,
In the wind,
You disappear,
To return to me Nevermore, Nevermore.

Chapter 6
Echoes of Memory

Spoken
Don't worry, about the lost they are not really gone
as long as you can remember them
they still live.

Chorus
Nothing is truly lost,
Nothing is truly gone,
All things lost still remain,
They still stay alive in memory,
of those who were there.

Verse
In the march of time,
People and things are lost,
Things always change,
For better or worse,

Chorus
Nothing is truly lost,
Nothing is truly gone,
All things lost still remain,
They still stay alive in memory,
of those who were there.

Verse
Dreams come and go,
People are taken by the gathering storm of time,
Eras change in the ebb and wane of time,
They are lost in the sands of time,

Chorus
Nothing is truly lost,
Nothing is truly gone,
All things lost still remain,
They still stay alive in memory,
of those who were there.

Coda
Nothing is truly lost,
Nothing is truly gone,
All things lost still remain,
They still stay alive in memory,
of those who were there.

Spoken
Everything remains in memory

Chapter 7
A Ghost of a Chance

Death has come to me,

I am still alive, but I know death has come for me.

I haven't a ghost of a chance to live,

I have only one last prayer to give,

On my life's blood, I wish to live on,

My life is almost gone,

I haven't a ghost of a chance to live,

I have only one last prayer to give,

I have one last breath to take

From this sleep, I won't awake.

Death has come to me,

I am still alive, but I know death has come for me.

I haven't a ghost of a chance to live,

I have only one last prayer to give,

On my life's blood, I wish to live on,

My life is almost gone,

I haven't a ghost of a chance to live,
I have only one last prayer to give,
I have one last breath to take
From this sleep, I won't awake.

Chapter 8

The Song of My Pen

My pen has a song that is its own,
words pour out of it like a song,
It is the music of words,
that come alive in its wake,
with every stroke of my pen, magic is performed,
a magical flow of words,
beauty and Gothic, happy and sad, which entice the heart and mind,
immaterial words of magical nature and life,
escape my pen and come alive.
In this material world,
of words and time.

Chapter 9
The Magicians song

You don't know the secrets beyond my smile,
I have a heart of darkness, I hide in plain sight,
You can't know my secret life beyond the light of day.

In the shadows of the night of my life,
I dwell in the shadows

Chapter 10

All we see or seem is but a dream within a dream book theme song v2

spoken plaintively

All we see or seem is but a dream within a dream

Chorus

My life is a series of secret lives,

I am more than what I seem,

no one sees who I truly am,

all they see is a dream of me,

All they see, or I seem, is but a dream within a dream

Verse

I am a mystery to the world,

I hide myself from the world,

I am just a dream to the world,

Chorus

My life is a series of secret lives,

I am more than what I seem,

no one sees who I truly am,

all they see is a dream of me,

All they see, or I seem, is but a dream within a dream,

Verse

They see me as many different men,

It is not fair they don't see me.

The truth they can't see,

Chorus

My life is a series of secret lives,

I am more than what I seem,

no one sees who I truly am,

all they see is a dream of me,

All they see, or I seem, is but a dream within a dream,

Coda

Like everyone else, all I see or seem is but a dream within a dream

All we see or seem is but a dream within a dream

Chapter 11
Where do dreams go when they die? - a Song

Spoken

Where do dreams go when they die?

Chorus

Where do dreams go when they die?

Where do dreams go when you lose them?

What happens when a memory dies?

Verse

They are lost and forgotten, but why?

They are lost to time,

They are merely forgotten memories.

Chorus

Where do dreams go when they die?
Where do dreams go when you lose them?
What happens when a memory dies?

Verse
Why do we lose our dreams?
Why do we forget them?
Where do dreams go?

Chorus
Where do dreams go when they die?
Where do dreams go when you lose them?
What happens when a memory dies?

Coda
Where do dreams go when they die?
Where do dreams go when they die?
Where do dreams go when they die?

Spoken
Why do dreams have to die?

Chapter 12
The Ravens

A flock of ravens floats upon the air over their prey,
Like a looming black storm cloud of gloom,
In the later hours of the death of the day,
They fight each other for room,
In the melee, one is injured it falls,
Blood and gore fill the air,
The air is filled with their dire calls,
Little did the observers of this carnage care,
To them, it was merely a display of the nature of the raven,
Upon the hour they fled,
They were neither crazed nor craven,
They were happy and well-fed.

Chapter 13
The Gothic Poets Department a song

Spoken

Welcome to The Gothic Poets Department,

Chorus

Welcome to The Gothic Poets Department, before you depart,

Home of the dark side of the art,

We all bear a dark heart,

Verse

Our founder of the league was Poe,

If we go to dark for you let us know,

we'll let you go,

Chorus

Welcome to The Gothic Poets Department, before you depart,

Home of the dark side of the art,

We all bear a dark heart,

Verse

We like the darkness of the night,

It really is a good sight,

though it causes in some great fright,

Chorus

Welcome to The Gothic Poets Department, before you depart,

Home of the dark side of the art,

We all bear a dark heart,

I know our art can scare some,

don't be glum,

not all to our art do succumb,

Chorus

Welcome to The Gothic Poets Department, before you depart,

Home of the dark side of the art,

We all bear a dark heart,

Chorus

Welcome to The Gothic Poets Department, before you depart,

We all bear a dark heart

Coda

Welcome to The Gothic Poets Department, before you depart,

We all bear a dark heart

Welcome to The Gothic Poets Department, before you depart,

Welcome to The Gothic Poets Department, before you depart,

(we part)
(we part)

Chapter 14

Shadows of the Forgotten Realm - song theme for Vivienne and the Reaper

Death has become real to me,

I am lost in the realm of darkness,

I am going to a place where the living all dread,

I am going to the realm of the dead,

I am becoming merely one of the

Shadows of the Forgotten Realm

I am in the Shadow lands of the dead,

I am lost in the realm of the dead,

fear and horror are my nearest and dearest friends here in the Shadows
of the Forgotten Realm.

Down here in the realm of the dead,

I fear where I'm going, I fear who I meet, I fear for my lost life in the
Shadows of the Forgotten Realm

Chapter 15
Death Called To Me

I wander lost and alone in a world I do not know,

Nobody sees or hears my cries,

I am dead, I know not,

where I am or where I will go,

I followed Death's call, and he left me alone and scared,

I don't know if he will come back for me,

I know not what am,

I know not where I go to,

I know not where this will end,

or if this solitary sentence will ever end

Chapter 16
Into The Fire

Intro

I shall walk into the fire,

I shan't stop,

Not now or ever,

Chorus

Give time reason and rhyme,

I shall continue on without fear or favour,

I shall go on into the fire,

I shall burn with ardour and confidence in me,

Verse 1

I shall move forwards,

I will not turn back,

No one can stop me

Meeting my fate,

I shall fight on,

Before it's too late,

Chorus

Give time reason and rhyme,

I shall continue on without fear or favour,

I shall go on into the fire,

I shall burn with ardour and confidence in me,

Verse 2

No one can stop me now,

I am on the road to my dream,

I won't stop now,

I will not hear the nay sayers,

I will fight on,

Chorus

Give time reason and rhyme,

I shall continue on without fear or favour,

I shall go on into the fire,

I shall burn with ardour and confidence in me,

Outro

I will never stop walking into the fire

Let the fire burn me,

I will see my dream to its end

Chapter 17

The Rose of Love

The Rose of love is on your cheeks,

I've seen it there for many weeks,

your eyes are like starlight on the water.

You are a dream to me, I saw you everywhere, but I never dreamed

you'd be mine, Oh stars daughter.

I never stopped loving you, though the years did part us,

For a spell, but our love is beyond life, death, and time's dusts

Chapter 18
Lost Dreams

Be I wish I could close my eyes and forget all the problems of life, the troubles that burn in my mind the sorrows, and the regrets gathered like flowers in the fields of life lived well, were there a balm of forgetfulness, I would consume it were it not death.

The flowers of hope and dreams grow in life's soils,

as I go through life's hardships and toils,

I wish I could close my eyes and forget all the problems of life, the troubles that burn in my mind the sorrows, and the regrets gathered like flowers in the fields of life lived well, were there a balm of forgetfulness, I would consume it were it not death.

I gather troubles like forget-me-nots and daisy chains,

they are life pains and banes,

I wish I could close my eyes and forget all the problems of life, the troubles that burn in my mind the sorrows, and the regrets gathered like flowers in the fields of life lived well, were there a balm of forgetfulness, I would consume it were it not death.

The flowers of hope and dreams grow in life's soils,

as I go through life's hardships and toils,

My hopes and cares would no longer there, they would fly away like
butterflies in the air,
Taking away my worries and cares
But it's like catching a snowflake, when you do, it's no longer there.

I wish I could close my eyes and forget all the problems of life

I wish I could close my eyes and forget all the problems of life,

Chapter 19
Shadows of Hell a song

Spoken dialogue
"The moon looks lovely tonight,"

Chorus
The moon is beautiful this night,
The night is quite a sight,
I could watch the moon all night,
Is that a falling star coming into sight,

Verse
I go see it where it fell,
I see it now well,
I see what befell,
It was a small UFO that fell,

Chorus
The moon is beautiful this night,

The night is quite a sight,
I could watch the moon all night,
Is that a falling star coming into sight,

Verse
Was their aliens inside,
What did inside abide,
I feared they had died,
The tiny little aliens climbed out the ship's side,

Chorus
The moon is beautiful this night,
The night is quite a sight,
I could watch the moon all night,
Is that a falling star coming into sight,

Chorus
The moon is beautiful this night,
The night is quite a sight,
I could watch the moon all night,
Is that a falling star coming into sight,

Spoken dialogue
"Where are you going?"
"I am going back to the garden,"
"Why?"
"I've got a date with the moon, it's a lovely night,"

Chapter 20

Behind His Blue Eye - Theme to The Magicians : Behind Blue Eyes

Spoken dialogue
"The moon looks lovely tonight,"

Chorus
The moon is beautiful this night,
The night is quite a sight,
I could watch the moon all night,
Is that a falling star coming into sight,

Verse
I go see it where it fell,
I see it now well,

I see what befell,
It was a small UFO that fell,

Chorus
The moon is beautiful this night,
The night is quite a sight,
I could watch the moon all night,
Is that a falling star coming into sight,

Verse
Was their aliens inside,
What did inside abide,
I feared they had died,
The tiny little aliens climbed out the ship's side,

Chorus
The moon is beautiful this night,
The night is quite a sight,
I could watch the moon all night,
Is that a falling star coming into sight,

Chorus
The moon is beautiful this night,
The night is quite a sight,
I could watch the moon all night,
Is that a falling star coming into sight,

Spoken dialogue

"Where are you going?"
"I am going back to the garden,"
"Why?"
"I've got a date with the moon, it's a lovely night,"

Chapter 21
The Magicians: The Ghost of Your Gaze or The Ghost's Serenade

Spoken
"What are you doing?"
"Why are you dressed
as the Ghost?"

Chorus
I'm a ghost,
I'm not ghosting you.
I am here, although you don't see me,
I am here, but you can't hear me,
All you see is another man,
With my face, and form,

Verse 1
You can see me through his facade,
I am the one how truly loves you,
but you see me as only a friend,
to you, I am merely a shade of myself.

Chorus
I'm a ghost,
I'm not ghosting you.
I am here, although you don't see me,
I am here, but you can't hear me,
All you see is another man,
With my face, and form,

Chorus
I'm a ghost,
I'm not ghosting you.
I am here, although you don't see me,
I am here, but you can't hear me,
All you see is another man,
With my face, and form,

Verse 2
Why can't you see me beyond the echos of the past,
Why are you blind to my love?
Will you ever see me?
The true me

Chorus

I'm a ghost,

I'm not ghosting you.

I am here, although you don't see me,

I am here, but you can't hear me,

All you see is another man,

With my face, and form,

Coda

I'm a ghost,

I'm not ghosting you.

I am here, although you don't see me,

I am here, but you can't hear me,

All you see is another man,

With my face, and form,

Spoken

"But you are no Ghost he is charming and amazing, you are just...

You."

"Well, I could be him, he is very

mysterious,"

Chapter 22

Left for dead book theme

They left me for dead

No one will find me here til I'm dead.
Why did they drive off,
leaving me here to die.
I was left for dead,
I was left for dead,
I was left to die,
I was here to lie.

I was left for dead,
I was left for dead,
I was left to die,
I was left here to lie.
I was left to die.
I was left to die alone,
I was left for dead,

I was left for dead,
I was left to die,
I was here to lie.

I was left for dead,
I was left for dead,
I was left to die,
I was left here to lie.
I was left to die.
I was left to die alone,
Why I was left to die?
I was wondering if will I ever be found.
I was hurt, scared, and alone.
I was left to die,
I was scared and alone to die,

Why?

Chapter 23

Death Has Come For Me

Death has come for me,
No one can cheat death,
not even death himself,
death has come for me,
No one can cheat death,
not even death himself,
There is no way back from
death once he has come for you.

Chapter 24

Masters of the Earth -The People From The Center of the Earth song theme

We are the star men

Chorus

We are the Star men,

masters of the Earth,

You can't take our place,

Verse

we run your world,

surface dwellers,

we own the earth

Chorus
We are the Star men,
masters of the Earth,
You can't take our place,
Verse
you can't take our place,
we live in your hollow planet,
we run your world without us
this planet will die.
Chorus
We are the Star men,
masters of the Earth,
You can't take our place,
Verse
we run your world,
surface dwellers,
we own the earth
Chorus
We are the Star men,
masters of the Earth,
You can't take our place.

Chapter 25

The Magicians: Pod Wars - The War is Live song

Spoken dialogue
"Welcome to the Blake and the Sandman podcast."
"have you heard of the Blake and the Sandman podcast?"
"I want you to do a podcast to rival it,"
"Welcome to the Daily Times podcast,
"Your podcast was garbage,"
"I told you I wouldn't be good,"
"Do better, or look for another job,"

Chorus
Welcome to the war,
The war is now live,
It is the Pod wars,
The war is on the air,

Verse 1
We'll do anything to win the war,
This Pod War,
We will not stop fighting until this war is done,

Chorus
Welcome to the war,
The war is now live,
It is the Pod Wars,
The war is on the air,

Verse 2
The war has only started,
This is only the beginning of the war,
You can not win this war,
Ratings are everything we care for,

Chorus
Welcome to the war,
The war is now live,
It is the Pod Wars,
The war is on the air,

Verse 3
You can not win this war no-matter who or what you are,
We will be the victor in this ratings war,
This war on the air,
You have no chance to win our war,

Chorus
Welcome to the war,

The war is now live,

It is the Pod Wars,

The war is on the air,

Coda
Welcome to the war,

The war is now live,

It is the Pod Wars,

The war is on the air,

Spoken
"Can you smell smoke?"

Chapter 26
A Darker Shade of Self - a song

Spoken
Know this that even saints have a shadow side to their hearts
it is but a darker shade of self

Chorus
Even saints have a shadow side to their hearts
it is but a darker shade of self,

Verse
This side may be hidden deep within their soul
deep down,
It is their other half, may be not always their better part,

Chorus
Even saints have a shadow side to their hearts
it is but a darker shade of self,

Verse
They may not even be aware of this darker shade
within their soul hidden deep within

Chorus
Even saints have a shadow side to their hearts
it is but a darker shade of self,

Chorus
Even saints have a shadow side to their hearts
it is but a darker shade of self,

Coda
Even saints have a shadow side

Even saints have a shadow side

it is but a darker shade of self,

it is but a darker shade of self

Chapter 27

Send in the Clowns book theme song

Send in the clowns,
The happy, friendly clowns,
Send in the clowns.
Masters of mirth and laughter,
Send in the clowns.
The happy, jolly clowns,
Send in the Clowns
We don't have any?
Send in the Clowns
These monsters anyway

Chapter 28
The Magicians: Disillusionment - song

Spoken

Why can't you see me?

I am not a dream,

I am not a fantasy

Look I am really here

Chorus

Why can't you see me beyond your dream of me,

I am not just a dream within your dream,

I am not a dream, I am me,

Verse

I am lost in your dreams,

You see me as a dream,

You know me am not a dream,

I am real.

Chorus

Why can't you see me beyond your dream of me,

I am not just a dream within your dream,

I am not a dream, I am me,

Verse

You know me,

I know you,

but why can't you see me

Chorus

Why can't you see me beyond your dream of me,

I am not just a dream within your dream,

I am not a dream, I am me,

Coda

Am not a dream

Spoken

Why can't you see me?

Chapter 29
The Magicians: Our Solemn Hour- Song

Spoken

Oh My God, what is that monster doing to that corpse?

It's coming back to life!

Chorus

I can't believe it,

I don't believe what I just saw!

I saw a dead man come back to life,

I know that man!

He can't be dead!

Verse

I saw him return to life but how?

What was that monster doing?

Was he the dead man somehow?

Chorus

I can't believe it,
I don't believe what I just saw!
I saw a dead man come back to life,
I know that man!
He can't be dead!
Verse
What can I do?
Who can I tell?
Will he come after me?
Chorus
I can't believe it,
I don't believe what I just saw!
I saw a dead man come back to life,
I know that man!
He can't be dead!
Coda
I can't believe it,
I don't believe what I just saw!
I saw a dead man come back to life,
I know that man!
He can't be dead!

Spoken
Dr Death came back to life
will he come for me?

Seven Pillars of Wisdom or Lawrence of Arabia His Life And Death: A poem

"The Lord is my light." He guided me all my life,
He guided me from birth and through my strife,
A Prince of men known and admired by all I call a friend,
I travelled to Arabia, which I alone defended,
I helped free Damascus from the Ottoman Turk,
Although some say I went berserk,

A free Arabia was always my dream,

After the war, I was accused of going Arab, or to them, it did seem,

I returned to real life and tried to hide,

My legend had grown too much for me to abide,

I could not be me!

Although the world could not see,

One day I rode hell for Leather on my motorcycle near Clouds Hill,

my home,

I had a serious accident, no longer did I roam,

I died and upon my grave, they wrote "Dominus illuminatio mea,"

"The Lord is my light." by those words my life did adhere.

About the author

Rachel is a lover of gothic
poetry and the stories of Emily Dickinson, Poe, and other poets and
writers. She writes in a gothic sometimes romantic, and somewhat
eclectic style

Is a classic, prolific writer.

Contact Rachel via her website

Where she writes
https://allpoetry.com/The_Poette

Good Reads Page
https://www.goodreads.com/author/show/17771936.Rachel_Laws
on

Website
http://www.rachellawsonpoet.yolasite.com/

YouTube songs are sung here

https://www.youtube.com/@BlakeAlexander-kq8qq

Spotify Artist Profile
https://open.spotify.com/artist/1G9bsRFWnpq2RgNcrJ7Jmw?si=S
vwykHkxQtGarCJM6Ijefw

Rachel Lawson, YouTube Topic
https://www.youtube.com/channel/UC2L3-DWz4IupjemyvNvfrw
A

Song Death Called to Me on YouTube
https://youtu.be/y9UcyVqiXjs

9 798224 037117